D0461537

Construction Vehicles at Work

BACKHOES

by Kathryn Clay

CAPSTONE PRESS
a capstone imprint

Little Pebble is published by Capstone Press,
1710 Roe Crest Drive, North Mankato, Minnesota 56003
www.mycapstone.com

Library of Congress Cataloging-in-Publication Data
Names: Clay, Kathryn, author.
Title: Backhoes / by Kathryn Clay.
Description: North Mankato, Minnesota : Capstone Press, [2017] | Series:
   Little pebble. Construction vehicles at work | Audience: Ages 4–8. |
   Audience: K to grade 3. | Includes bibliographical references and index.
Identifiers: LCCN 2015048720| ISBN 9781515725275 (library binding) |
ISBN 9781515725329 (pbk.) | ISBN 9781515725374 (ebook pdf)
Subjects: LCSH: Backhoes—Juvenile literature.
Classification: LCC TA735 .C584 2017 | DDC 629.225—dc23
LC record available at http://lccn.loc.gov/2015048720

Editorial Credits
Erika L. Shores, editor; Juliette Peters and Kayla Rossow, designers;
Eric Gohl, media researcher; Tori Abraham, production specialist

Photo Credits
Alamy: B Christopher, 19, Frank Paul, 15; iStockphoto: Dr-Strangelove, 9, ewg3D, 21, gece33, 11, studio9400, 5; Shutterstock: Dmitry Kalinovsky, cover, 1, 7, Ivto, 17, TFoxFoto, 13

Design elements: Shutterstock

Printed in China.
007704

Table of Contents

About Backhoes

Look!

Here comes a backhoe.

It is also called a digger.

See the long arm?

It is called a boom.

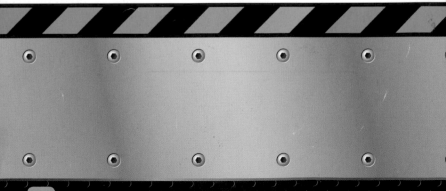

boom

Booms go up and down.

The bucket digs and scoops.

bucket

Buckets have sharp teeth.

They break up big rocks.

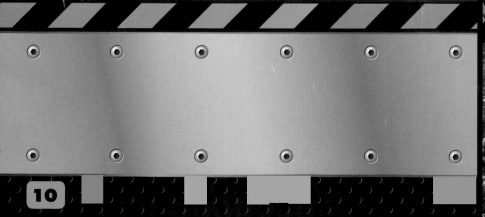

teeth

See the big blade?

It is called a loader.

It moves dirt.

loader

Joe is the driver.

He sits in the cab.

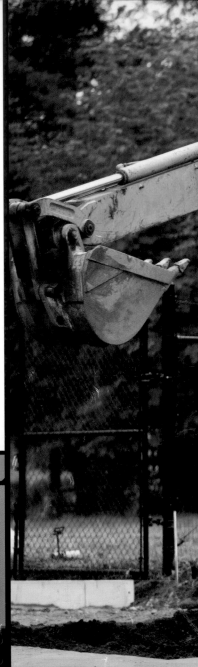

cab

At Work

A digger makes
a big hole.
Water pipes are put
in the ground.

A digger makes
land smooth.
Workers build
a new road.

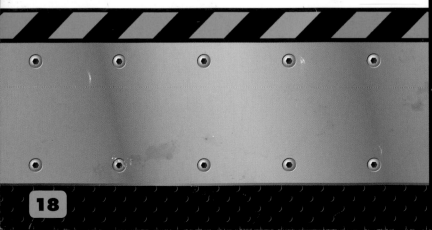

A digger clears
trees and rocks.
Workers build
a new house.

Good job, digger!

Glossary

blade—a wide, curved piece of metal; the blade pushes, scrapes, and picks up rocks and dirt

cab—the place where the driver sits

smooth—even and free from bumps

Read More

Alinas, Marv. *Diggers*. Big Machines at Work. North Mankato, Minn.: The Child's Word, 2014.

Gifford, Clive. *Diggers and Cranes*. Machines at Work. St. Catharines, Ontario: Crabtree Publishing Company, 2013.

Meister, Cari. *Backhoes*. Machines at Work. Minneapolis: Jump, 2014.

Internet Sites

FactHound offers a safe, fun way to find Internet sites related to this book. All of the sites on FactHound have been researched by our staff.

Here's all you do:
Visit *www.facthound.com*
Type in this code: 9781515725275

Super-cool stuff! Check out projects, games and lots more at **www.capstonekids.com**

Index